BIOGRAPHY O ... ROBERTS

CW00495204

Exploring the Life and Times of the
Leading Woman in Hollywood

ELSIE CHRISTIAN

All rights reserved. No part of this publication may be reproduced, distributed, or transmitted in any form or by any means, including photocopying, recording, or other electronic or mechanical methods, without the prior written permission of the publisher, except in the case of brief quotations embodied in critical reviews and certain other noncommercial uses permitted by copyright law.

© ELSIE CHRISTIAN, 2024.

TABLE OF CONTENTS

INTRODUCTION

In the sunny town of Smyrna, Georgia, a shining star named Julia Fiona Roberts came into the world on October 28, 1967. Little did anyone know that this small-town girl would grow up to become a Hollywood sensation, enchanting audiences worldwide with her charm and talent. Julia's journey is not just a Hollywood tale but a story of determination, resilience, and the pursuit of dreams.

Born into a warm family, Julia's childhood was filled with laughter and play, laying the foundation for a future that would see her conquer the silver screen. From the streets of New York City to auditions and rejections, her early years in the industry were marked by a relentless pursuit of her passion. Julia's rise to stardom was not without its challenges, but each setback only fueled her determination to prove herself.

The 1990s marked the pinnacle of Julia's career, with iconic roles that left an indelible mark on cinema. From the vivacious Vivian Ward in "Pretty Woman" to the tenacious Erin Brockovich, Julia's performances transcended the screen, resonating with audiences worldwide. Beyond the glitz of Hollywood, she emerged as a woman of substance, navigating personal challenges while using her fame to champion social causes close to her heart.

As we delve into the pages of this biography, be prepared for a captivating journey through the life and times of Julia Roberts. From the quaint streets of Smyrna to the dazzling lights of Tinseltown, her story is a celebration of dreams, resilience, and the magic that happens when a small-town girl's laughter echoes through the history of cinema. Get ready to be spellbound by the extraordinary life and enduring legacy of Julia Roberts, a name forever etched in the brightest moments of the silver screen.

Chapter 1: Childhood and Family Background.

On a crisp autumn day, October 28, 1967, in the quiet suburb of Smyrna, Georgia, Julia Fiona Roberts made her debut into the world, bringing with her the promise of a future marked by stardom and acclaim. Born to Betty Lou Bredemus and Walter Grady Roberts, Julia was the youngest member of a family whose roots traced a diverse and fascinating heritage.

The Roberts family tree bore the branches of English, Scottish, Irish, Welsh, German, and Swedish ancestry, creating a rich tapestry of cultural influences that would later shape Julia's identity. Raised in a household where her father identified as Baptist, her mother as Catholic, and Julia herself embraced the Catholic faith, she was exposed to a harmonious blend of religious beliefs.

Betty Lou and Walter Grady Roberts were not merely Julia's parents; they were also one-time actors and playwrights with a shared love for the performing arts. Their paths crossed during theatrical productions for the United States Armed Forces, and this shared passion blossomed into a lasting partnership. The couple went on to co-found the Atlanta Actors and Writers Workshop, an institution that became a hub for artistic expression in Midtown Atlanta.

The Roberts family's involvement in the arts extended beyond their professional endeavors. During Betty Lou's pregnancy with Julia, the couple ran a children's acting school in Decatur, Georgia, highlighting their commitment to nurturing young talent. Notably, the children of Coretta and Martin Luther King Jr. were among the students at this school. Walter Roberts, in particular, served as an acting coach for Yolanda King, the daughter of the iconic civil rights leaders. In a touching display of gratitude, Coretta King paid the Roberts family's hospital bill when Julia was born, recognizing Walter's role in running the only racially integrated theater troupe in the region.

However, the idyllic image of family life underwent a significant transformation. In 1972, Julia's parents, who had married in 1955, faced the difficult decision to part ways. Betty Lou filed for divorce in 1971, and the divorce was finalized in early 1972. This marked a pivotal moment in Julia's life, leading to a period of adjustment and change.

From 1972 onward, Julia resided in Smyrna, Georgia, attending Fitzhugh Lee Elementary School, Griffin Middle School, and Campbell High School. Her mother remarried in the same year to Michael Motes, a chapter in Julia's life marked by challenges. Motes, often unemployed and abusive, strained the family dynamics, leading to a turbulent relationship with Julia. The union produced a daughter, Nancy Motes, whose life ended tragically at the age of 37 due to a drug overdose in 2014.

The complexities of Julia Roberts' family history extend further with the passing of her own father, Walter Grady Roberts, when she was just ten years old. This early loss undoubtedly left an indelible mark on her life and shaped the woman she would become.

Julia Roberts' birth and family background thus serve as a compelling prologue to the remarkable journey that unfolded in the years to come. The blend of diverse ancestry, the influence of theatrical pursuits, and the challenges faced within the family dynamic all contributed to the multifaceted personality that would later grace screens worldwide.

Educational Background.

Julia Roberts' educational journey and early interests paint a vivid picture of a young woman whose intellect and curiosity were as vibrant as her on-screen presence. Following her formative years in Smyrna, Georgia, Julia embarked on an academic path that, while diverging from the conventional, ultimately laid the groundwork for her iconic career.

After completing her early education at Fitzhugh Lee Elementary School, Griffin Middle School, and Campbell High School in Smyrna, Julia's interests extended beyond the conventional academic pursuits. Notably, she harbored childhood aspirations of becoming a veterinarian, a testament to her love for animals and nature. This early dream hinted at a compassionate side to the young Julia, foreshadowing her later involvement in philanthropy and advocacy for animal welfare.

Julia's engagement with the arts was not confined to the theatrical world her parents inhabited. She was an active participant in her school's band, playing the clarinet. This musical pursuit showcased her versatility and love for creative expression, laying the foundation for a well-rounded approach to her future endeavors.

Upon completing her high school education in Smyrna, Julia took a unique turn in her academic journey. Rather than following a traditional path to higher education, she enrolled at Georgia State University, located in Atlanta. However, her time at the university did not culminate in a degree, as the allure of the performing arts beckoned her elsewhere.

Driven by her passion for acting, Julia made the bold decision to venture to the bustling metropolis of New York City. It was here, amidst the towering skyscrapers and the pulsating heartbeat of Broadway, that she sought to carve her niche in the world of acting. The decision marked a pivotal moment in her life, setting the stage for a career that would see her ascend to the pinnacle of Hollywood stardom.

In the bustling atmosphere of New York City, Julia signed with the Click Modeling Agency, a move that hinted at her striking beauty and potential as a model. Simultaneously, she enrolled in acting classes, honing her craft and preparing for the challenges of the competitive entertainment industry. This period of transition and self-discovery in the city that never sleeps marked the beginning of a chapter that would propel Julia Roberts into the limelight.

Julia's educational background, while unconventional in its trajectory, reflects the dynamic and exploratory nature of her early years. Her journey from a small town in Georgia to the vibrant cityscape of New York embodies the spirit of a woman unafraid to forge her own path.

Chapter 2: Entry into Acting.

Julia Roberts' entry into the realm of acting was a multi-faceted journey that began with a combination of family influence, early exposure, and a genuine passion for the craft. Her parents, Betty Lou Bredemus and Walter Grady Roberts, were not only her guardians but also pivotal figures in the world of theater and acting.

Julia's parents, who initially connected through their shared love for the performing arts, set the stage for her early exposure to the world of acting. Their involvement in theatrical productions for the United States Armed Forces led them to co-found the Atlanta Actors and Writers Workshop, where they created an environment that fostered artistic expression. As a child, Julia found herself immersed in this creative atmosphere, surrounded by the captivating energy of the stage.

During her mother's pregnancy, the Roberts family ran a children's acting school in Decatur, Georgia. This experience not only underscored the family's commitment to the arts but also introduced Julia to the magic of storytelling and performance at a tender age. The fact that the children of Coretta and Martin Luther King Jr. were among the students in their school speaks to the inclusive and impactful nature of the Roberts family's contribution to the arts.

Julia's first notable television appearance occurred in 1987 on the series "Crime Story." In the episode titled "The Survivor," she portrayed a juvenile rape victim, showcasing her ability to tackle emotionally challenging roles even at the outset of her career. This marked a pivotal moment as it propelled her from the realms of family influence to the broader world of professional acting.

Simultaneously, Julia made her big-screen debut in the dramedy "Satisfaction" (1988), where she played a band member in search of a summer gig. This transition to film represented a significant step, signaling her intent to explore acting beyond the familial environment. Her entry into the cinematic world showcased her ability to navigate both the small and big screens, setting the stage for a versatile and enduring career.

In the same year, she appeared in the fourth-season finale of "Miami Vice," broadening her exposure to diverse genres and platforms. However, it was her role in the independent romantic comedy "Mystic Pizza" (1988) that marked her first critical success with audiences. Julia portrayed a Portuguese-American teenage girl working as a waitress, earning praise for her performance from critics like Roger Ebert, who recognized her as a "major beauty with a fierce energy."

Julia Roberts' entry into acting was characterized by a seamless blend of family influence, early exposure, and an innate talent that quickly garnered attention. From her early days in television to her breakthrough in independent cinema, each step in her journey contributed to the evolution of a star who would go on to define an era in Hollywood. Her entry into acting wasn't just a career choice; it was the beginning of a legacy that continues to captivate audiences worldwide.

Breakthrough Moment.

Julia Roberts' role in the film "Steel Magnolias" (1989) was a defining moment in her career, showcasing her exceptional acting prowess and earning her critical acclaim along with a string of accolades. In this film adaptation of Robert Harling's play of the same name, Roberts portrayed the character of Shelby Eatenton Latcherie, a young bride grappling with diabetes in a close-knit Southern community.

Shelby's character was complex, requiring depth and nuance to bring her to life. The film delved into the challenges Shelby faced due to her health condition, highlighting her resilience, determination, and the deep bonds she shared with the women in her life. Julia Roberts' portrayal of Shelby was marked by a perfect blend of vulnerability and strength, capturing the hearts of audiences with her authentic and emotionally charged performance.

The narrative of "Steel Magnolias" revolved around the intertwining lives of a group of Southern women, exploring themes of friendship, love, and the enduring strength of the female spirit. Julia Roberts played a pivotal role in shaping the emotional core of the movie, with her character's journey serving as a focal point for the audience's emotional investment.

Critically, Julia Roberts' performance was widely praised. Despite being a relative newcomer in Hollywood, she held her own among seasoned co-stars such as Sally Field, Dolly Parton, Shirley MacLaine, and Daryl Hannah. Director Herbert Ross, known for being demanding on set, pushed Roberts to deliver a standout performance. Sally Field later acknowledged that Ross "went after Julia with a vengeance" since "Steel Magnolias" was essentially her first major film. Nevertheless, Julia rose to the occasion, infusing Shelby with a radiant charm that made her both relatable and memorable.

The film, upon its release, received acclaim from critics and audiences alike. Julia Roberts' performance earned her the first Academy Award nomination of her career, nominated for Best Supporting Actress. In addition to the Oscar nomination, she won the Golden Globe Award for Best Supporting Actress in a Motion

Picture, solidifying her status as a rising star in Hollywood.

"Steel Magnolias" proved to be both a critical and commercial success. Audiences were captivated by the powerful performances, and the film resonated deeply, particularly due to its poignant exploration of friendship and the emotional landscape of women facing life's challenges. The movie's success at the box office, coupled with the recognition Julia Roberts received for her role, marked a pivotal moment in her career, setting the stage for the unparalleled success she would achieve in the following years.

In essence, Julia Roberts' role in "Steel Magnolias" not only demonstrated her acting prowess but also played a crucial role in elevating the film to iconic status. The critical acclaim, coupled with the commercial success, showcased her ability to command attention on the big screen and foreshadowed the illustrious career that would unfold in the decades to come.

Chapter 3: Iconic Roles in the 90s

Pretty Woman 1990

Julia Roberts' role in "Pretty Woman" (1990) marked a defining moment in her career and remains one of the most iconic performances in the history of romantic comedies. Her portrayal of Vivian Ward, an assertive and compassionate freelance hooker with a heart of gold, not only elevated the film to unprecedented success but also solidified Julia Roberts as a global superstar.

The narrative of "Pretty Woman" follows the Cinderella–Pygmalionesque storyline, where Roberts' character, Vivian, crosses paths with wealthy businessman Edward Lewis, played by Richard Gere. What initially begins as a business arrangement evolves into a heartwarming tale of love, transformation, and self-discovery.

Julia Roberts brought a perfect blend of vulnerability, charm, and strength to the character of Vivian. Her magnetic on-screen presence and infectious energy infused the film with a captivating authenticity that resonated with audiences worldwide. The chemistry between Roberts and Richard Gere was palpable, creating an enchanting dynamic that became the soul of the movie.

Roberts' acting in "Pretty Woman" played a pivotal role in shaping the film's narrative. Vivian's journey from a woman surviving on the streets to finding love and self-worth was anchored by the depth and nuance that Roberts infused into the character. Her ability to convey a range of emotions, from defiance and resilience to vulnerability and tenderness, made Vivian a multi-dimensional and relatable protagonist.

Critically, Julia Roberts received widespread acclaim for her performance. Critics lauded her charisma, calling her the "soul" of the film. Her portrayal of Vivian Ward showcased a breakthrough combination of humor, strength, and vulnerability, demonstrating her versatility as an actress. Audiences were captivated by her genuine and heartfelt performance, which played a significant role in the film's immense popularity.

"Pretty Woman" became a cultural phenomenon and a box office sensation. The film saw the highest number of ticket sales in the U.S. ever for a romantic comedy, breaking records and surpassing expectations. Globally, it made an astounding $463.4 million, solidifying its status as one of the highest-grossing romantic comedies of all time.

Beyond the box office success, the red dress that Julia Roberts wore in the film became an iconic symbol of cinematic fashion. The movie's impact extended beyond the theaters, influencing fashion trends and leaving an indelible mark on popular culture.

Julia Roberts' performance in "Pretty Woman" earned her a second Academy Award nomination, this time for Best Actress, and a second Golden Globe Award win for Best Actress in a Motion Picture (Musical or Comedy). Her portrayal of Vivian not only showcased her acting prowess but also served as a testament to her ability to anchor a film and resonate with audiences on a profound level.

In summary, Julia Roberts' role in "Pretty Woman" was a tour de force that elevated the film to legendary status. Her stellar performance, coupled with the enchanting narrative and on-screen chemistry with Richard Gere, contributed to the film's critical acclaim and unprecedented commercial success. "Pretty Woman" not only solidified

Julia Roberts as a Hollywood icon but also left an enduring legacy in the romantic comedy genre.

Flatliners

Julia Roberts' role in the film "Flatliners" (1990) marked a departure from her previous romantic comedy success and showcased her versatility as an actress in the supernatural thriller genre. Directed by Joel Schumacher, the film explores the consequences of experimenting with near-death experiences and delves into the psychological complexities of its characters.

In "Flatliners," Roberts played the character of Rachel Mannus, one of five medical students engaged in a daring experiment to explore the afterlife by inducing near-death experiences. The narrative unfolds as the characters, led by Kiefer Sutherland's Nelson Wright, embark on a journey to probe the mysteries of death and beyond. Roberts' portrayal of Rachel is integral to the film's exploration of guilt, redemption, and the haunting consequences of past actions.

Rachel Mannus, portrayed by Julia Roberts, is haunted by the memory of an accident in which she inadvertently caused the death of a young boy while driving. The character grapples with intense guilt and seeks resolution through the risky experiment of flatlining. Roberts' nuanced performance conveys the emotional weight of Rachel's guilt, fear, and desire for redemption, adding layers of complexity to the character.

Julia Roberts' acting played a crucial role in shaping the film's narrative, particularly in conveying the psychological and emotional toll of the characters' experiences. As the narrative unfolds, Rachel's journey becomes a focal point, and Roberts skillfully navigates the character's internal struggles, making her a compelling and empathetic figure for the audience.

"Flatliners" received a polarized critical reception upon its release. While some critics praised the film's psychological depth and suspenseful atmosphere, others found fault in its execution and pacing. Roberts' performance, however, was generally well-received, with many acknowledging her ability to infuse the character of Rachel with a sense of vulnerability and emotional authenticity.

The film's commercial performance was moderate, achieving profitability at the box office. Over time, "Flatliners" has gained a cult following, with audiences appreciating its exploration of existential themes and psychological horror elements. Julia Roberts' contribution to the film's success lies in her ability to bring emotional depth to the narrative and engage viewers in the characters' complex moral dilemmas.

In retrospect, Julia Roberts' role in "Flatliners" showcased her willingness to take on diverse and challenging roles, breaking away from the romantic comedy genre that initially defined her career. While the film faced mixed critical reception, Roberts' performance as Rachel Mannus demonstrated her range as an actress and her capacity to elevate the emotional resonance of a film. "Flatliners" remains a notable entry in Julia Roberts' filmography, marking a phase in her career where she ventured into uncharted territories and continued to evolve as a versatile and accomplished performer.

Diversity across Genres

Julia Roberts' roles in the films "Sleeping with the Enemy" (1991), "Hook" (1991), and "Dying Young" (1991) showcased her versatility as an actress across different genres. Each film presented unique challenges and narratives, allowing Roberts to explore a range of characters and emotions.

In "Sleeping with the Enemy," directed by Joseph Ruben, Julia Roberts played the role of Laura Burney, a woman attempting to escape an abusive marriage. The film navigates the psychological thriller genre as Laura fakes her death to start a new life. Roberts' portrayal of a battered wife seeking freedom was a departure from her previous roles, and her performance added depth to the character. The film received mixed reviews from critics, with some praising Roberts' convincing portrayal and the film's suspenseful elements. Commercially, it grossed $175 million worldwide, proving to be a box office success.

In Steven Spielberg's fantasy film "Hook," Julia Roberts took on the whimsical role of Tinkerbell, a winged, six-inch-tall fairy. The film is a modern adaptation of J.M. Barrie's classic tale of Peter Pan. Roberts' performance as Tinkerbell, alongside Robin Williams and Dustin Hoffman, contributed to the film's magical atmosphere. While the critical reception was mixed, with some praising the visual effects and performances, others found fault in the narrative. Commercially, "Hook" was a significant success, grossing $300.9 million worldwide.

"Dying Young" (1991):
In "Dying Young," directed by Joel Schumacher, Julia Roberts played the role of Hilary O'Neil, an outgoing yet cautious nurse who cares for a young man with leukemia, portrayed by Campbell Scott. The film explored themes of love, illness, and personal growth. Roberts' performance received mixed reviews from critics, with praise for her chemistry with Campbell Scott but criticism for the film's predictability. Commercially, it grossed $82.3 million globally.

In each of these films, Julia Roberts' acting shaped the narrative by bringing authenticity and emotional depth to her characters. In "Sleeping with the Enemy," her portrayal added a layer of realism to the thriller, making the audience empathize with the character's plight. In "Hook," her whimsical and enchanting performance as Tinkerbell contributed to the film's fairy-tale ambiance. "Dying Young" showcased Roberts' ability to convey the emotional complexities of a character dealing with love and illness.

While critical reception varied for each film, Julia Roberts' performances were consistently praised. Her star power and ability to connect with audiences played a crucial role in the commercial success of these films. The diverse roles she undertook in this period highlighted her willingness to take on challenging projects and explore different facets of her acting capabilities.

Overall, Julia Roberts' contributions to "Sleeping with the Enemy," "Hook," and "Dying Young" further solidified her standing as one of Hollywood's leading actresses, capable of taking on a range of roles across genres and captivating audiences with her talent and charisma.

Following a two-year hiatus from the screen, Julia Roberts returned with the legal thriller "The Pelican Brief" (1993), co-starring Denzel Washington. The film, based on John Grisham's novel, was a commercial hit, grossing $195.2 million worldwide. However, her subsequent films, including "I Love Trouble" (1994), "Prêt-à-Porter" (1994), and "Something to Talk About" (1995), received mixed reviews and moderate box office returns.

In the mid-1990s, Julia Roberts experienced a career resurgence with a series of romantic comedies. In "My Best Friend's Wedding"

(1997), she played a food critic trying to win back her best friend, marking one of the best romantic comedies of all time. The film was a global box office hit, grossing $299.3 million. Her next film, "Conspiracy Theory" (1997), a political thriller with Mel Gibson, earned a respectable $137 million.

In 1998, Julia Roberts showcased her versatility by starring in the drama "Stepmom," exploring the complex relationship between a terminally-ill mother and her future stepmother. While reviews were mixed, the film grossed $159.7 million worldwide.

The late 1990s continued to see Roberts thrive in the romantic comedy genre. "Notting Hill" (1999), where she starred opposite Hugh Grant, surpassed "Four Weddings and a Funeral" as the biggest British hit in cinema history, earning $363 million worldwide. Her reunion with Richard Gere and Garry Marshall in "Runaway Bride" (1999) also achieved financial success, grossing $309.4 million globally.

Throughout this period, Julia Roberts' star power remained unparalleled, and her contributions to both critical and commercial successes solidified her legacy as one of the most influential actresses in Hollywood. Her ability to seamlessly transition between genres and captivate audiences across the globe marked a remarkable chapter in her illustrious career.

Chapter 4: Iconic Roles(2000s)

"Erin Brockovich" (2000)

In the film "Erin Brockovich" (2000), Julia Roberts took on the formidable role of real-life legal crusader Erin Brockovich, a tenacious environmental activist fighting against the Pacific Gas and Electric Company. Roberts' portrayal skillfully shaped the narrative by bringing Erin's character to life with a perfect blend of resilience, determination, and charisma. The film follows Erin's journey as she uncovers corporate wrongdoing and fights for justice, showcasing her evolution from a struggling single mother to a formidable force challenging a powerful corporation.

Julia Roberts' performance in "Erin Brockovich" is hailed as one of her career-defining roles. Her ability to embody the emotional depth of Erin, while also portraying her wit and tenacity, earned her widespread acclaim. The nuanced portrayal of Erin's struggles, both personally and professionally, resonated with audiences and critics alike. Roberts' convincing and powerful performance in the lead role earned her the Academy Award for Best Actress, marking a historic achievement as the first actress to command a $20 million salary for a film.

The critical reception for Julia Roberts' performance in "Erin Brockovich" was overwhelmingly positive. Critics lauded her ability to capture the essence of Erin, emphasizing the emotional toll of her journey as she balances the responsibilities of a single mother with her fight for justice. Peter Travers of Rolling Stone praised Roberts for showcasing the "emotional toll on Erin," and Entertainment Weekly's Owen Gleiberman found delight in watching Roberts bring a "flirtatious sparkle" with an undertow of melancholy. The film's success was undeniably tied to Roberts' compelling portrayal of the titular character.

"Erin Brockovich" not only received critical acclaim but also achieved remarkable success at the box office. The film resonated with audiences worldwide, grossing an impressive $256.3 million globally. The combination of a compelling narrative, a real-life underdog story, and Julia Roberts' award-winning performance contributed to the film's commercial triumph. "Erin Brockovich" became a cultural touchstone, cementing its place in cinematic history as a socially relevant and commercially successful film.

America's Sweethearts and The Mexican

In "America's Sweethearts," Julia Roberts took on a comedic role as Kiki Harrison, the once-overweight sister and assistant to a glamorous Hollywood actress. Roberts' portrayal shaped the narrative by infusing humor and charm into the character, navigating the complexities of the entertainment industry. The film explores the dynamics between celebrities, their personal lives, and the challenges of maintaining public images, with Roberts contributing to the lighthearted yet insightful storytelling.

While the film boasted a star-studded cast, including John Cusack, Billy Crystal, and Catherine Zeta-Jones, critics noted a lack of sympathetic characters in the production. Despite this, Julia Roberts received praise for her performance, with her comedic timing and relatable portrayal of Kiki earning positive reviews. The critical consensus acknowledged Roberts' contribution to the film's entertainment value, even if the overall reception was mixed.

"America's Sweethearts" achieved notable success at the box office, grossing over $138 million worldwide. The film's commercial performance was buoyed by the audience's interest in the comedic exploration of Hollywood's behind-the-scenes dynamics and the chemistry among the ensemble cast. Julia Roberts' presence undoubtedly contributed to the film's appeal, showcasing her ability to draw audiences in both dramatic and comedic roles.

In "The Mexican," Julia Roberts starred alongside Brad Pitt in a road gangster comedy. The film's narrative revolves around a script originally intended as an independent production that eventually attracted A-list actors like Roberts and Pitt. Roberts' character, Samantha Barzel, plays a pivotal role in the unfolding events as her relationship with Pitt's character intertwines with the comedic and dramatic elements of the story.

"The Mexican" received mixed reviews from critics who noted that, despite being advertised as a romantic comedy, the film did not focus solely on the actors' relationship. Julia Roberts and Brad Pitt shared relatively little screen time together, leading to varying opinions on the film's overall tone. While the critical reception was not overwhelmingly positive, Roberts received acknowledgment for her performance, and her collaboration with Pitt garnered attention.

The film performed moderately well at the North American box office, grossing $66.8 million. While not a blockbuster, the movie's commercial success can be attributed to the star power of Roberts and Pitt, drawing audiences curious about their on-screen collaboration. Despite the mixed critical reception, the film's box office performance indicated the audience's interest in the unconventional storyline and the chemistry between the two lead actors.

Ocean Eleven

In "Ocean's Eleven," Julia Roberts took on the role of Tess Ocean, the ex-wife of George Clooney's character, Danny Ocean. Roberts' acting played a crucial part in shaping the narrative, as her character becomes entangled in the elaborate heist orchestrated by Danny and his team. The subplot involving Tess adds a layer of complexity and emotion to the film, creating a dynamic where personal relationships intersect with the high-stakes world of heist planning. Roberts' performance brings both elegance and depth to Tess, making her a pivotal element in the intricate storytelling.

The critical reception for Julia Roberts' role in "Ocean's Eleven" was largely positive. Critics praised the ensemble cast, highlighting the chemistry between Roberts and Clooney. While some critics noted that her character's role in the heist plot was relatively understated compared to other team members, Roberts' presence and performance were consistently commended. The film's overall critical success was attributed to the charismatic performances of the cast, including Roberts, which contributed to the film's enjoyable and stylish atmosphere.

"Ocean's Eleven" emerged as a major commercial success, grossing a staggering $450 million worldwide. Audiences were drawn to the combination of star power, intricate plot twists, and the heist genre's appeal. Julia Roberts' involvement, along with the ensemble cast, undoubtedly played a significant role in attracting audiences. The film's box office triumph solidified it as one of the highest-grossing films of the year, showcasing the widespread popularity of the heist caper and the star-studded ensemble.

While "Ocean's Eleven" didn't result in major awards for Julia Roberts individually, the film's success contributed to its lasting legacy. The chemistry between Roberts and Clooney, along with the overall charm of the cast, turned the film into a modern classic within the heist genre. The film's success paved the way for sequels and reinforced Julia Roberts' standing as part of a cinematic phenomenon that resonated with audiences worldwide.

"Mona Lisa Smile"

In "Mona Lisa Smile" Julia Roberts tackled the role of Katherine Ann Watson, an art history professor at Wellesley College in the conservative 1950s. Roberts' portrayal shaped the narrative by embodying Watson's progressive ideals and challenging societal norms. As a teacher who encourages her students to question traditional roles for women, Roberts' character becomes a catalyst for change within the restrictive academic and social environment. Watson's journey, guided by Roberts' nuanced performance, underscores themes of female empowerment, intellectual freedom, and the pursuit of individual fulfillment.

The critical reception for Julia Roberts' role in "Mona Lisa Smile" was mixed, with opinions often centered on the film's predictability and its safe approach to addressing societal issues. However, Roberts received praise for her convincing portrayal of a forward-thinking educator committed to empowering her students. While critics acknowledged the film's formulaic elements, Roberts' performance was often cited as a standout, with her on-screen presence contributing to the film's overall appeal.

"Mona Lisa Smile" achieved moderate success at the box office, grossing over $141 million worldwide. The film's exploration of gender roles and societal expectations resonated with audiences, and Julia Roberts' star power likely contributed to drawing viewers. While not a blockbuster, the film's financial performance indicated its capacity to attract audiences interested in thought-provoking narratives centered on women's empowerment and societal change.

Despite mixed critical reviews, "Mona Lisa Smile" has left a lasting impact on discussions surrounding gender roles and education. Julia Roberts' portrayal of Katherine Ann Watson added a compelling dimension to the film, emphasizing the importance of challenging societal expectations. The movie's themes of individualism, intellectual freedom, and the pursuit of one's passions have contributed to its enduring relevance, making it a notable entry in Roberts' filmography.

The mid-2000s saw Julia Roberts expanding her repertoire, voicing characters in animated films like "The Ant Bully" (2006) and "Charlotte's Web" (2006). Her Broadway debut in "Three Days of Rain" received mixed reviews, showcasing her versatility beyond the screen. In "Charlie Wilson's War" (2007), Roberts delivered a compelling performance as socialite Joanne Herring, earning her a sixth Golden Globe nomination.

"Fireflies in the Garden" (2008), an independent drama, allowed Roberts to explore a mother's complex emotions. Although the film faced delayed North American release, it demonstrated her commitment to diverse and challenging roles. In the comic thriller "Duplicity" (2009), Roberts showcased her evolution as an actress, receiving praise for her strategic use of mannerisms. Despite mixed reviews, her performance earned her a seventh Golden Globe nomination.

"August: Osage County"

In the star-studded ensemble cast of "August: Osage County," Julia Roberts emerged as a formidable force, portraying Barbara

Weston-Fordham, a pivotal character in this emotionally charged drama.

Roberts tackled the complexity of her character with finesse, depicting Barbara as a woman grappling with family dysfunction, personal crises, and the weight of responsibility. Her compelling portrayal allowed the audience to witness the evolution of a daughter confronting her own demons while navigating the tumultuous dynamics of her family.

Critics lauded Roberts for her powerful performance, noting her ability to convey the raw intensity of the character's emotional journey. The film, directed by John Wells and based on Tracy Letts' Pulitzer Prize-winning play, earned praise for its honest portrayal of familial struggles. Roberts' nuanced acting contributed significantly to the movie's critical acclaim.

"August: Osage County" resonated with audiences who appreciated its exploration of complex relationships and the impact of buried secrets. While not a blockbuster, the film's box office performance was solid, bolstered by its strong ensemble cast, including Meryl Streep and Ewan McGregor. Roberts' presence added a layer of authenticity to the familial narrative, enhancing the film's appeal.

For her role as Barbara, Julia Roberts received several award nominations, including an Academy Award nomination for Best Supporting Actress. The film itself garnered multiple nominations, showcasing the collective strength of the cast and crew.

In the 2010s, Julia Roberts not only maintained her status as one of Hollywood's highest-paid actresses but also ventured into roles that showcased her versatility and ability to draw audiences across genres. From environmental activism to heist capers,

Roberts continued to shape her legacy as an iconic figure in the film industry.

Wonder (2017)

In the heartwarming film "Wonder," Julia Roberts took on the role of Isabel Pullman, a mother navigating the challenges of raising a son with Treacher Collins syndrome, a rare craniofacial condition. Roberts' portrayal of a supportive and resilient mother played a pivotal role in shaping the film's narrative.

Roberts brought a delicate balance of strength and vulnerability to Isabel Pullman, portraying a mother fiercely protective of her son, Auggie, while grappling with societal prejudices and her own fears. The character, as brought to life by Roberts, became the emotional anchor of the film, guiding the audience through a journey of acceptance, compassion, and understanding.

Critics praised Roberts for her heartfelt performance, acknowledging her ability to convey the emotional intricacies of a parent facing extraordinary circumstances. The film, directed by Stephen Chbosky and based on R.J. Palacio's bestselling novel, received acclaim for its sincere exploration of themes like bullying, acceptance, and the transformative power of kindness. Roberts' nuanced portrayal significantly contributed to the positive critical reception.

"Wonder" resonated with audiences seeking a poignant and uplifting narrative. Roberts' star power, coupled with a compelling story, contributed to the film's success at the box office. The movie's commercial performance reflected its universal appeal and the emotional connection viewers formed with the characters, particularly Roberts' portrayal of Isabel.

While Julia Roberts did not receive individual award nominations for her role in "Wonder," the film itself received positive attention. The movie's impact on audiences, coupled with critical acclaim, affirmed its place as a significant contribution to the genre of family dramas.

In "Wonder," Julia Roberts brought depth and authenticity to the character of Isabel Pullman. Her role as a nurturing and resilient mother elevated the film, making it a touching exploration of love, acceptance, and the beauty found in our differences.

"Mirror Mirror"

As the Wicked Queen, Roberts infused the character with a delightful mix of wit, cunning, and theatrical flair. Her interpretation of the classic fairy-tale antagonist added layers to the narrative, creating a character both menacing and oddly captivating. Roberts' performance became a centerpiece, driving the plot forward through her character's intricate schemes and interactions with Snow White.

Critics celebrated Roberts' deliciously wicked performance, noting her ability to inject humor and complexity into a character often portrayed in a more one-dimensional light. The film's lighter and more comedic take on the Snow White tale, coupled with Roberts' charismatic portrayal, received praise for offering a fresh perspective on the classic story. The actress's playful approach to the role contributed significantly to the critical acclaim.

"Mirror Mirror" found success at the box office, with audiences drawn to the film's visually stunning presentation and Roberts' standout performance. The movie's commercial performance benefited from Roberts' star power, attracting viewers with its whimsical take on the familiar fairy-tale narrative. The film's global box office success reflected its broad appeal and Roberts' contribution to its marketability.

Julia Roberts' portrayal of the Wicked Queen in "Mirror Mirror" showcased her versatility as an actress. By infusing the character with a blend of humor and malice, Roberts added a memorable dimension to the film. The Wicked Queen became more than just a fairy-tale antagonist; she became a captivating and entertaining force driving the story forward.

While not a traditional retelling of the Snow White story, "Mirror Mirror" left an impression on audiences who appreciated its unique spin. Julia Roberts' performance as the Wicked Queen added a layer of sophistication to the film, proving that even in a fantastical realm, her acting prowess could elevate a character beyond expectations.

In "Mirror Mirror," Julia Roberts embraced the whimsy of fairy-tale villainy, creating a character that stood out for its complexity and humor. Her role as the Wicked Queen contributed to the film's success, making it a noteworthy addition to the diverse landscape of Snow White adaptations.

In her television debut with "Homecoming," Roberts took on the role of Heidi Bergman, a caseworker in a psychological thriller. This marked a departure from her usual cinematic ventures, and Roberts seamlessly adapted to the episodic format. Her captivating performance brought psychological depth to the series, creating suspense and intrigue. Critics lauded Roberts for her nuanced portrayal, and her Golden Globe nomination for Best Actress underscored the success of her foray into television.

Chapter 5: Beyond the Silver Screen.

Julia Roberts, known for her radiant smile on screen, has had a noteworthy journey in her personal life. The actress has been married twice. Her first marriage was to country singer Lyle Lovett in 1993, a union that surprised many due to their diverse backgrounds. Unfortunately, the marriage was short-lived and ended in 1995. Roberts then found enduring love with cinematographer Daniel Moder, whom she married in 2002. The couple shares three children and their enduring relationship has been a source of tabloid fascination, admired for its stability in the often tumultuous world of Hollywood relationships.

Beyond her stellar acting career, Julia Roberts has carved a prominent place for herself in the realm of philanthropy and social causes. Her commitment to various charitable organizations showcases her desire to make a positive impact beyond the silver screen. Roberts has been an advocate for environmental issues, supporting initiatives that focus on conservation, sustainable living, and the fight against climate change. The actress has been actively involved in campaigns related to health and education, particularly those aimed at improving access to healthcare and education for underprivileged communities. Roberts has shown a particular interest in supporting children's causes. Her involvement in organizations dedicated to child welfare and rights highlights her commitment to creating a better future for the younger generation. In memory of her "The Normal Heart" co-star, Roberts has contributed to the fight against HIV/AIDS. Her involvement in awareness campaigns and fundraising efforts reflects a commitment to addressing health crises on a global scale.

Awards and Recognition

Julia Roberts, with her magnetic performances and undeniable talent, has garnered a multitude of awards and accolades throughout her illustrious career. Her journey in the world of cinema has not only made her a beloved actress but has also solidified her as one of the most decorated figures in Hollywood.

Roberts' pinnacle achievement came with the Academy Awards. She clinched the Oscar for Best Actress for her role in "Erin Brockovich" (2000). Her portrayal of real-life environmental activist Erin Brockovich earned her critical acclaim, and the coveted statuette was a testament to her exceptional acting prowess. The Golden Globes have been a frequent stage for Roberts' triumphs. She secured her first Golden Globe for Best Supporting Actress in "Steel Magnolias" (1989), followed by a win for Best Actress in a Motion Picture (Musical or Comedy) for her iconic role in "Pretty Woman" (1990). Roberts continued her streak, clinching another Golden Globe for "Erin Brockovich."

The British Academy of Film and Television Arts recognized Roberts with the BAFTA Award for Best Actress in a Leading Role for "Erin Brockovich." This international acknowledgment underscored the global impact of her performance. Roberts has been honored by her peers at the SAG Awards. She received the Outstanding Actress in a Leading Role award for "Erin Brockovich," further solidifying her standing among fellow actors. While primarily known for her film career, Roberts ventured into television with "The Normal Heart" (2014). Her powerful performance in this HBO film earned her a Primetime Emmy Award nomination for Outstanding Supporting Actress in a Miniseries or a Movie.

In recognition of her enduring contributions to the entertainment industry, Julia Roberts was honored with a star on the Hollywood Walk of Fame in 2000. This coveted star stands as a tangible testament to her lasting impact on Hollywood. Roberts' popularity among audiences is evident in her multiple People's Choice Awards. Whether it's Favorite Movie Actress or Favorite Dramatic Movie Actress, these awards reflect the public's unwavering admiration for her work.

Beyond the realm of entertainment, Roberts received the Global Philanthropy Award in 2010 from the Swedish World Childhood Foundation. This award acknowledged her dedication to philanthropic endeavors and humanitarian causes.

Conclusion

Julia Roberts, a name that has resonated through decades of cinema, stands as an enduring icon of longevity in the ever-evolving landscape of Hollywood. Her career, marked by a multitude of accolades, awards, and iconic roles, is a testament to both her exceptional talent and the rare ability to connect with audiences across generations.

From the early years of "Mystic Pizza" (1988) to the Oscar-winning triumph of "Erin Brockovich" (2000), Roberts has navigated the dynamic currents of the film industry with grace and prowess. Her longevity is not just measured in the span of her career but in the profound impact she has left on the cinematic landscape.

Roberts' ability to seamlessly transition between genres, from romantic comedies like "Pretty Woman" (1990) to intense dramas like

"Steel Magnolias" (1989) and "Erin Brockovich," showcases a versatility that few actors possess. Her longevity is not rooted solely in the number of years she's spent in the limelight but in the diverse array of characters she's brought to life.

The awards adorning her illustrious career – the Academy Award, Golden Globe, BAFTA, and SAG Awards – are not just symbols of recognition but milestones in a journey marked by excellence. Yet, beyond the glittering trophies, Roberts' star on the Hollywood Walk of Fame, received in 2000, speaks to a lasting legacy etched into the very fabric of the entertainment industry.

Her foray into television with "The Normal Heart" (2014) and her more recent roles in films like "Wonder" (2017) and the series "Homecoming" (2018) further underscore her adaptability and relevance in an industry that constantly evolves.

Julia Roberts' longevity is not confined to the silver screen; it's a reflection of her enduring appeal, her ability to resonate with audiences of different ages and backgrounds. She isn't just an actress; she's a cultural touchstone, an embodiment of timeless talent that defies the passage of years.

Printed in Great Britain
by Amazon

42820269R00036